Sleep Deprivation
& Its Consequences

...NG ADULT'S GUIDE TO THE SCIENCE OF HEALTH

Allergies & Asthma

Contraception & Pregnancy

Coping with Moods

Dental Care

Drug- & Alcohol-Related Health Issues

Fitness & Nutrition

Growth & Development

Health Implications of Cosmetic Surgery,
Makeovers, & Body Alterations

Healthy Skin

Managing Stress

Sexually Transmitted Infections

Sleep Deprivation & Its Consequences

Smoking-Related Health Issues

Suicide & Self-Destructive Behaviors

Weight Management

Young Adult's Guide to the Science of Health

Sleep Deprivation
& Its Consequences

Joan Esherick

MASON CREST

Mason Crest
450 Parkway Drive, Suite D
Broomall, PA 19008
www.masoncrest.com

Printed in the Hashemite Kingdom of Jordan.

First printing
9 8 7 6 5 4 3 2 1

Series ISBN: 978-1-4222-2803-6
Hardcover ISBN: 978-1-4222-2815-9
Paperback ISBN: 978-1-4222-3003-9
ebook ISBN: 978-1-4222-9011-8

The Library of Congress has cataloged the
    hardcopy format(s) as follows:

        Library of Congress Cataloging-in-Publication Data

Esherick, Joan.
  Sleep deprivation & its consequences / Joan Esherick.
     pages cm. – (Young adult's guide to the science of health)
  Audience: 12.
  Audience: Grade 7 to 8.
  Includes bibliographical references and index.
  ISBN 978-1-4222-2815-9 (hardcover) – ISBN 978-1-4222-2803-6 (series) – ISBN 978-1-4222-9011-8 (ebook) – ISBN 978-1-4222-3003-9 (paperback)
  1. Insomnia–Juvenile literature. 2. Sleep deprivation–Juvenile literature. 3. Teenagers–Sleep. I. Title. II. Title: Sleep deprivation and its consequences.
  RC548.E76 2014
  616.8'4982–dc23
                    2013006391

Designed and produced by Vestal Creative Services.
www.vestalcreative.com

This book is meant to educate and should not be used as an alternative to appropriate medical care. Its creators have made every effort to ensure that the information presented is accurate and up to date—but this book is not intended to substitute for the help and services of trained medical professionals.

Contents

Introduction

by Dr. Sara Forman

You're not a little kid anymore. When you look in the mirror, you probably see a new person, someone who's taller, bigger, with a face that's starting to look more like an adult's than a child's. And the changes you're experiencing on the inside may be even more intense than the ones you see in the mirror. Your emotions are changing, your attitudes are changing, and even the way you think is changing. Your friends are probably more important to you than they used to be, and you no longer expect your parents to make all your decisions for you. You may be asking more questions and posing more challenges to the adults in your life. You might experiment with new identities—new ways of dressing, hairstyles, ways of talking—as you try to determine just who you really are. Your body is maturing sexually, giving you a whole new set of confusing and exciting feelings. Sorting out what is right and wrong for you may seem overwhelming.

Growth and development during adolescence is a multifaceted process involving every aspect of your being. It all happens so fast that it can be confusing and distressing. But this stage of your life is entirely normal. Every adult in your life made it through adolescence—and you will too.

But what exactly is adolescence? According to the American Heritage Dictionary, adolescence is "the period of physical and psychological development from the onset of puberty to adulthood." What does this really mean?

In essence, adolescence is the time in our lives when the needs of childhood give way to the responsibilities of adulthood. According to psychologist Erik Erikson, these years are a time of separation and individuation. In other words, you are separating from your parents, becoming an individual in your own right. These are the years when you begin to make decisions on your own. You are becoming more self-reliant and less dependent on family members.

When medical professionals look at what's happening physically—what they refer to as the biological model—they define the teen years as a period of hormonal transformation toward sexual maturity, as well as a time of peak growth, second only to the growth during the months of infancy. This physical transformation from childhood to adulthood takes place under the influence of society's norms and social pressures; at the same time your body is changing, the people around you are expecting new things from you. This is what makes adolescence such a unique and challenging time.

Being a teenager in North America today is exciting yet stressful. For those who work with teens, whether by parenting them, educating them, or providing services to them, adolescence can be challenging as well. Youth are struggling with many messages from society and the media about how they should behave and who they should be. "Am I normal?" and "How do I fit in?" are often questions with which teens wrestle. They are facing decisions about their health such as how to take care of their bodies, whether to use drugs and alcohol, or whether to have sex.

This series of books on adolescents' health issues provides teens, their parents, their teachers, and all those who work with them accurate information and the tools to keep them safe and healthy. The topics include information about:

- normal growth
- social pressures
- emotional issues
- specific diseases to which adolescents are prone
- stressors facing youth today
- sexuality

The series is a dynamic set of books, which can be shared by youth and the adults who care for them. By providing this information to educate in these areas, these books will help build a foundation for readers so they can begin to work on improving the health and well-being of youth today.

A Sleepy Society: Why Teens Don't Get Enough Sleep

The pulsating beep of her alarm clock startled seventeen-year-old Sarah out of her deep slumber. *I can't believe it's five o'clock already,* the teen moaned to herself as she hit the snooze button on the top of her digital clock. *It feels like I just went to bed—I DID just go to bed,* she realized as she remembered her late night studying. *Four hours ago. I only got four hours of sleep. And I have to work today, too. It's going to be a long day.*

Rolling onto her back, she reached up to flip on the reading light clipped to her bed's headboard. She squeezed her eyes tight at the sudden glare of the 100-watt bulb.

I guess I should get up, Sarah thought to herself, then pulled

the quilted comforter up tighter to her chin. *But it's so warm in here, and it's so cold out there. Maybe I'll just rest a minute longer. Just another minute or two.*

The next thing she knew, her alarm was sounding again. The clock read 5:15 a.m.

I've got to get up, but I'm so tired. Just a little more sleep. Just a little more...

The clock read 5:30 a.m. when Sarah woke next.

"Arrrrrgggg! It's already 5:30! Now I won't have time for a full workout at the gym," she mumbled as she whipped her covers off and scrambled to the bathroom.

Sleep Deprivation & Its Consequences

Sleepy Teens

Do you ever feel like Sarah? Exhausted, needing more sleep, but frustrated when you get up late? If you do, you're not alone. A recent study by the National Sleep Foundation (NSF) found that 60 percent of people under the age of eighteen complained of daytime tiredness. Fifteen percent (one out of every seven) said they were so tired they fell asleep in school. Additional NSF data suggests that adolescents simply don't get enough sleep:

Around 10 percent of students surveyed typically slept less than six hours per night on weekdays, with only 15 percent reporting that they slept more than eight and a half hours. Eighty percent of the high school students in a different study stated that they went to bed after 11:00 p.m. on weekends and weeknights. It's no wonder kids complain of being tired. They are!

Kids aren't alone in their exhaustion. A 2008 study reports 29 percent of adults felt very sleepy or fell asleep at work in the past month. Thirty-two percent drive drowsy at least one to

ARE YOU SLEEP DEPRIVED?

The NSF publication entitled *Adolescent Sleep Needs and Patterns* lists four signs of sleep deprivation in teens:

1. Difficulty waking up in the morning.
2. Grumpiness and irritability later in the day.
3. Unintentionally falling asleep during the day.
4. Sleeping more than usual on the weekends.

If these describe you, you may be dangerously sleep deprived.

two times per month. Thirty-six percent have nodded off or fallen asleep while driving—a situation that can have deadly results. The National Highway Traffic Safety Administration (NHTSA) estimates that drowsy driving causes over 100,000 automobile accidents each year, resulting in some 71,000 injuries and 1,550 fatalities annually.

Why are we so sleepy? We just don't get enough zzzz's.

It's estimated that adolescents require more sleep than they did as pre-adolescents, sometimes as much as nine and a quarter hours per night. One study by the NIH found that when adults were allowed to sleep without interruption, on average they slept eight to eight and a half hours at one time. Teens slept closer to just over nine hours. Researchers have determined from these studies that the average sleep requirement of teenagers is eight and a half to nine and a quarter hours per night. Anything less than that produces **CHRONICALLY** sleepy teens.

Sleepiness is nothing more than your body crying out for something it needs. If your body needs food, it tells you by giving you hunger pangs or a growling stomach. If your body needs water, it communicates its need by making you thirsty. And if your body needs sleep, it lets you know by making you feel sleepy.

SLEEPY TEENS A GREATER PROBLEM EACH YEAR

According to the U.S. Census Bureau, the number of teens ages fifteen to nineteen is expected to rise to 26.5 million by 2050. That means more sleepy teens!

Sleep, just like food and water, is a **BIOLOGICAL NEED**, and your body will tell you when it's not getting enough.

At its root, sleepiness is your body's reaction to not getting sufficient sleep—a condition called being sleep deprived. The problem in America is that most people don't take sleep deprivation seriously.

The 24/7 Society

In recent years, the term "24/7" has become a popular phrase in North America. Most teens know that "24/7" originated as short-hand for saying "twenty-four hours a day, seven days a week," especially for instant messaging on the Internet. The fact that such a phrase even exists indicates just how busy we are. We weren't always this busy.

Before the invention of electricity and the light bulb, people went to bed not long after the sun went down at night, and got up when the sun rose in the morning. Thanks to Ben Franklin and Thomas Edison, however, the sun no longer dictates when

AVERAGE SLEEP NEEDS BY AGE

Newborns (0-2 months): 12-18 hours

Infants (3-11 months): 14-15 hours

Toddlers (1-3 years): 12-14 hours

Preschoolers (3-5): 11-13 hours

School-age (5-10): 10-11 hours

Teens (10-17): 8.5-9.25 hours

Adults: 7-9 hours

(From www.sleepfoundation.org)

Sleep Deprivation & Its Consequences

we sleep and when we rise. We can be up and active twenty-four hours a day.

And, truth be told, we want to be. We like being busy, so we pack our days full of activities and responsibilities. Consider exhausted Sarah's schedule on the day she overslept (if sleeping in until 5:30 a.m. can even be called oversleeping!) Here's what she planned to do that day:

5:00–5:30 a.m.: Get up, brush teeth, feed cat, get gym stuff together, drive to gym.

5:30–6:30 a.m.: Work out at gym (swim, do weights).

6:30–7:00 a.m.: Shower and dress for school.

7:00–7:15 a.m.: Drive to school.

7:15 a.m.–2:45 p.m.: Attend school.

2:45–3:00 p.m.: Drive home.

3:00–3:45 p.m.: Get snack, change into work clothes, look at homework.

3:45–4:00 p.m.: Drive to work.

4:00–7:15 p.m.: Work

7:15–7:30 p.m.: Drive home, grab dinner.

7:30–9:00 p.m.: Change clothes, do part of homework.

9:00–11:00 p.m.: Go out with friends.

11:00 p.m.–1:00 a.m.: Go home, do rest of homework.

1:00 a.m.: Go to bed.

And the next day her schedule started all over again at 5:00 a.m. after only four short hours of sleep. Sarah's day, which included only working out, school, her part-time job, homework, and time with friends doesn't seem unreasonably busy. Even if she'd skipped going out with friends, she still wouldn't have gotten to bed until after 11:00 p.m. And consider that her schedule allowed no time for breakfast (which she regularly skipped), less than fifteen minutes for dinner, no time for after-school ac-

tivities (like sports team participation, dances, committees, or football games), no time for chatting with friends on the computer or talking on the phone, and only brief, in-passing interaction with her family. On days that she tries to cram any of these things in, too, she gets even less sleep.

You may object that Sarah invests three and a half hours of homework per night, when not all students do. But national statistics suggest that her volume of homework isn't unusual for a high school student. Honors, gifted, or advanced placement students invest even more time in their studies. Now imagine the student who, in addition to a part-time job and schoolwork, marches in a marching band, swims on a swim team, or plays

Many North Americans—including teens—don't value bedtime as an important part of their schedules. As a result, sleep is not a priority in their lives.

Sleep Deprivation & Its Consequences

Q & A

Q: Why are we so sleepy?
  A: *Because we don't get enough sleep.*

Q: Why don't we get enough sleep?
  A: *Because we don't view sleep to be as important as the other things we do.*

football or lacrosse. These students run from the moment they get up in the morning until they drop into bed at night. And most don't get nearly enough sleep. Yet they wouldn't change what they do. They enjoy it too much.

Teens, like everyone else, have only twenty-four hours in a day. They do what they must (going to school, for example, which is required by law) plus what they want to do (for example, going out with friends). What happens when they don't have time to do all they'd like to do? They cut the least urgent thing in their schedules, and that is usually sleep. Sleep doesn't feel that important to teenagers, so it is often sacrificed first. Dr. James P. Kiley, Director of the National Center on Sleep Disorders Research, explains, "…we have a society that's on a 24-hour cycle—with multiple jobs in many cases and multiple responsibilities both at work and home. When you're pushed for time, as many people are, the first thing that usually goes is sleep." Everything else seems like a higher **PRIORITY** because society tells us it is, and because we misunderstand the importance and nature of sleep.

Busyness = Importance?

Cliff is President of the Student Council, an honors student, and lead scorer on the water polo team. Outgoing and friendly, he's one of the most popular kids in school.

Rochelle is the quiet, studious type. She loves to read, and her only school activity is contributing articles to the school newspaper about community events.

Sean is a loner at school. He has few friends, no activities, and struggles to get through his classes. He spends his weekends home alone in his room, watching TV or playing games on the computer.

Question: Which student is more important? Which has greater value?

Answer: None of them. They all have an **INTRINSIC** worth, just because they are who they are.

People in America today live in a fast-paced, breathless society—a culture that applauds busyness and productivity. We

URGENT OR IMPORTANT?

Teens often sacrifice sleep because the need for sleep seems less urgent than the need to be with friends or do homework or earn extra money. But urgency does not always equal importance. Consider these definitions:

Urgent: pressing, insistent
Important: essential, vital

Getting homework done or earning money isn't imperative for a teen's health or survival; but sleep is. Which is more important?

The pressures of a busy schedule often interfere with getting enough sleep.

think we find our worth in how much we do or in how much we perform. We mistakenly assume that full calendars make us important or more valuable than the next guy. If we have nothing to do, we're either completely bored, feel restless, think we're useless, or feel **DEFECTIVE**. Teens, especially, don't want to admit they have nothing happening on a Friday night or weekend; it makes them feel like misfits or outcasts. Something must be wrong, it's sometimes assumed, with a teenager who isn't busy or has few friends.

What is the source of your value? Your busyness—or who you are inside?

Sleep Deprivation & Its Consequences

Nothing could be further from the truth. Think about it for a moment. If we think our value comes from how well we play basketball or from how many things we have on our activity plates, what happens when those things are taken away? What happens to the basketball player who breaks his neck in a diving accident and can't play ball anymore? Is he of any less value than he was before? Of course not! He's the same person inside! Only his abilities have changed. Or what happens to the over-achieving teenager who's on a gazillion committees, is an honor student, and has a job, but then loses her mother to breast cancer and has to cut back on her activities to help out at home? Does she have any less worth because she can't be on student council anymore? Again, of course not. Her value isn't based on how many committees she serves on; it's based on the fact that she is a human being with a value, worth, and dignity that comes with being human alone, just as the former basketball star is. These teens' importance has nothing to do with what they do or how full their calendars are; they are valuable simply because they exist—it's who they are that makes them special; not what they do.

Collectively, as a culture, Americans have overemphasized the importance of busyness and lost sight of the value of rest. We've begun to value people for what they do (instead of who they are). Since sleep doesn't produce measurable results, we undervalue the role sleep plays in our health and well-being. It is, after all, only sleep. And we can certainly live without that, right?

Wrong.

We'll address the nature and importance of sleep (what it is, what it does for us) and why we can't live without it in the next chapter, but let's talk about busyness for a moment more. According to the National Institutes of Health (NIH), problem sleepiness in adolescents is the pattern of insufficient, irregular, and poorly timed sleep.

A SLEEPY SOCIETY: Why Teens Don't Get Enough Sleep

THINGS THAT INFLUENCE TEEN SLEEP PATTERNS

- lessening parental control
- increasing peer influence
- school starting times
- job hours
- additional responsibilities
- health factors (diet, exercise, etc.)
- biological delays in sleep timing (teens tend to fall asleep later)
- stress

How We Spend Time Is a Choice!

None of us wakes up one day suddenly too busy to sleep. As small children, we had time to take naps and go to bed early because our parents or guardians made responsible choices (hopefully) about the use of our time. They made sure we got enough rest to stay healthy, often because if we didn't get enough sleep they paid for our sleeplessness by having to put up with our exhaustion-induced grumpiness or frequent colds and other infections. They knew that well-rested children made happy, healthy children, so they put us to bed when we needed to sleep, even when we didn't want to go.

But parents don't put adolescents to bed, and that's how it should be. Part of growing up is learning to manage time independently, and adolescents need to learn how to juggle schedules and manage their rest. It's all part of the process of becoming an adult.

Sleep Deprivation & Its Consequences

What most adolescents (and many adults) don't realize, however, is that every "yes" to one activity necessarily means "no" to something else. When we say "yes" to taking a part-time job after school, for example, we simultaneously say "no" to after-school activities. When we say "yes" to taking advanced placement courses and the extra homework these courses require, we say "no" to having that much more time with friends. When we say "yes" to participating in a varsity sport, we say "no" to all

Trying to fit EVERYTHING into twenty-four hours can make you stressed and confused!

the things we could have done in the time spent working out with the team. Every "yes" also means "no" in that we can't be in two places at once. Minutes can only be spent one time; we can never get them back again.

86,400 Seconds to Spend as You Wish

It's like we're all given a bank account, but not an account filled with money; it's an account filled with time. These bank accounts start fresh each day with twenty-four hours (1440 minutes or 86,400 seconds). When we "spend time" doing something (seven hours at school, three hours at work, two hours playing computer games or watching TV) we reduce our time accounts by that much. For many teens, their time accounts are spent on so many other things that little is left for sleep. Sarah, who opened this chapter, spent twenty hours of her daily time account on school, work, friends, driving, and other miscellaneous things, which left only four hours in her account for sleep. And, like it or not, she couldn't borrow from yesterday or tomorrow. Sarah was stuck with four hours of sleep because of how she chose to spend her time. We're each given only twenty-four hours in a day.

We are largely sleep deprived today because we don't really see sleep as that important, and because of how we choose to use our time. We will discuss time management issues in this book's last chapter, but it's important to understand that for most of us, sleep deprivation is a reversible condition. It can be changed and overcome. We don't have to live as chronically sleepy people, but can choose to live differently.

We won't choose to allow time in our budgets for sleep, however, until we begin to value sleep as not only important but necessary and beneficial for our well-being. In order to do that, we need to understand what sleep is and what it does for us, and what going without sleep can cost us in the long run.

2

THE SCIENCE OF SLEEP:
How Does Sleep Work
and What Does It Do for Us?

Is this statement true or false? *Sleep is the time during which our bodies and minds become inactive in order to give us rest.*

If you said "true," you would be wrong. The correct answer is false.

Our bodies may be still when we sleep, but our minds are far from being inactive. Sleep actually is a time of much physical and biological activity, which involves several body systems, the most active of which is the brain. We didn't always know this to be true.

WHEN IS SLEEP SLEEP?

How do you tell the difference between sleep, coma, unconsciousness, and death? For sleep to be sleep, by medical definition, it must be marked by these two characteristics:

1. The part of our brains that interacts with the world around us (our conscious minds) must be unaware of and not PERCEIVE the outside world.
2. The condition of unawareness must be immediately reversible. We must be able to wake up.

For thousands of years, until the 1950s in fact, scientists and PHILOSOPHERS considered sleep to be a time when all consciousness and brain activity stopped. Just as the body was usually still during sleep (eyes closed, body resting), people assumed the brain was still, too. With the discovery of certain technologies, including the electroencephalograph (EEG) machine, which tracks electrical signals in the brain, and the polysomnograph, which monitors brain signals as an EEG does plus other body functions like heart and breathing rates, scientists learned that sleep is a time of very high brain activity.

By using EEG and polysomnograph technologies, sleep researchers identified five distinct stages of sleep, all of which are necessary to recharge our bodies. These stages make up what sleep researchers call our sleep architecture.

If you think of the design of an ordinary house—its architecture—you'll realize a house is often made up of five basic things (in its simplest form): a foundation, walls, doors, windows, and a roof. Without any one of these structures, the architecture of

Sleep Deprivation & Its Consequences

the house would be incomplete. Researchers tell us now that in a similar way, all five stages of sleep work together to make up the complete architecture of sleep. Without any one of these stages, sleep's architecture would be incomplete.

The Stages of Sleep

Shortly after we go to bed at night we drift into the first stage of sleep. Stage One sleep is that drowsy, **TRANSITIONAL** stage when you move from being awake to being asleep. Have you ever watched someone fall asleep? His eyelids may have drooped or grown heavy, his muscles may have begun to relax, his breathing may have slowed, and he may have been less aware of what was going on around him. You knew he was falling asleep, but if you woke him just then, he may have denied he was sleeping. That person was in Stage One sleep.

Stage One is a state from which you can be easily awakened. It usually lasts ten minutes or less, rarely longer. It's the time when you feel yourself drifting away to slumber land. Sounds in the room may appear to echo or grow more distant, but you can still hear them. You will generally either wake from Stage One sleep or move to Stage Two. You won't linger in the first stage of sleep very long.

Stage Two sleep is seen by many people as the first true sleep state because it's the time when we're no longer aware of our surroundings. Stage Two sleep occurs when our heart rates slow even more, our breathing rates decrease, our eyes stop moving, we become completely relaxed, and we've tuned out the outside world. Though we are truly asleep, we can still be easily awakened from Stage Two. This second stage of sleep lasts twenty to fifty minutes per cycle, and comprises nearly 50 percent of our overall sleep for one night. From here we move to Stage Three.

STAGE OF SLEEP	CHARACTERISTICS	AVERAGE TIME spent in this stage per sleep cycle (amounts in each stage vary with each successive cycle)
Stage One	Light sleep marked by drowsiness, heavy eyelids, relaxed muscles, slowed heart and breathing rates, vague awareness of surroundings, and ease of waking	Ten minutes or less
Stage Two	What many people think of as first true sleep state, light sleep marked by closed eyes, no eye movement, slower heart and breathing rates, deeply relaxed muscles, no awareness of surroundings, slower brain waves, and ease of waking	Twenty to fifty minutes (we spend nearly fifty percent of our sleep time here)
Stage Three	Deep sleep state reached twenty minutes after lying down that transitions quickly to next stage marked by progressively more of the slower brain waves (delta waves) no eye movement, less muscle activity, and difficulty waking	Twenty minutes – (rapidly transition from this stage to the next)
Stage Four	Deepest sleep state marked by no eye movement, only delta waves, no muscle activity, and extreme difficulty waking	Twenty to thirty minutes
REM Sleep	Lighter sleep when most dreams occur and when eyes move rapidly beneath the lids	Ten to sixty minutes (as little as ten minutes during the first sleep cycle to as much as sixty minutes after eight or nine hours of sleep)

Stage Three is a rapidly deepening sleep stage through which we pass from Stage Two to Stage Four. Stages Three and Four are the deepest levels of sleep and the hardest from which to wake. On an EEG machine, Stages Three and Four show up as "delta waves" or slow wave sleep, which reflects the deepest level of unconsciousness while sleeping. Delta wave sleep is the kind of sleep that provides the rest our bodies and minds need to be restored. When we get enough delta wave sleep, we wake up feeling refreshed and energized.

We arrive in Stage Three sleep roughly twenty minutes after falling into the earliest part of Stage One sleep, and move progressively into Stage Four, the deepest sleep stage, over the next thirty or forty minutes. It takes, on average, just over one hour to move from Stage One to Stage Four sleep.

One characteristic these first four stages hold in common is the stillness of our eyes through each stage. Because our eyes don't tend to move during these stages, these four quieter stages of sleep are called Non-Rapid Eye Movement (NREM) sleep. During the fifth and final phase of sleep, called Rapid Eye Movement (REM) sleep, our eyes dart back and forth under our eyelids, indicating that our brains are very active. REM sleep is a lighter sleep stage during which nearly all dreaming occurs.

We enter Stage Five, or REM sleep, about ninety minutes after we fall asleep. We first pass through Stages One, Two, Three, and Four, experiencing the deepest levels of sleep first, then return to the lighter REM sleep and begin dreaming. Our minds

Sleep Deprivation & Its Consequences

start sorting through and **CONSOLIDATING** memories during this phase and it's from this stage's brain activity that dreams are generated. Scientists feel that REM sleep is critical for maintaining healthy minds.

Interestingly enough, though our minds are most active during Stage Five (REM) sleep, our bodies (with the exception of our eyes, hearts, lungs, nasal tissues, and **ERECTILE** tissues) remain still during this stage. Have you ever awakened during a dream and been unable to move or call out? That's because you woke during REM sleep. Your body is essentially paralyzed during REM sleep. This temporary paralysis is the way the body protects itself while the brain is active. Our heart and breathing rates may increase during REM sleep, but our muscles stay still. Imagine if your body physically acted out the movements of your dreams. Not only would your body be unable to rest if it weren't paralyzed, but you might hurt yourself.

Five Stages = One Sleep Cycle

When we pass through all five stages of sleep, the first four NREM stages, plus the fifth REM stage, sleep researchers say that we've completed one sleep cycle. It takes only ninety to one hundred and ten minutes, on average, to complete one full sleep cycle, so most people go through at least four or five cycles per night. After completing the first cycle, the next cycle is measured from the end of our first REM sleep through all the sleep stages again to the end our next REM sleep. The third cycle occurs from the end of our second REM sleep to the end of our third, and so on. Cycling through each of the stages several times in a given night is what allows us to awaken feeling refreshed, recharged, and ready for the day.

Not all sleep cycles, however, are the same. The typical first sleep cycle contains very little REM sleep, but longer periods of

ANOTHER SLEEP TURN-ON

Neurotransmitters aren't the only substance the body produces to signal us to fall asleep. A hormone called melatonin does the same thing. Melatonin production is stimulated by the absence of light. When the sun goes down, your brain produces melatonin, telling your body to go to sleep. When the sun comes up and when you're flooded by light all day long, melatonin production nearly stops all together, sending the message that it's time to be awake.

deep sleep. As the night progresses, the REM sleep periods increase with each cycle, moving to as much as sixty minutes in length by morning, while deep sleep stages shorten. The National Institute on Neurological Disorders and Stroke estimates that after a good night's sleep, most people will have spent the majority of their sleep time in Stage Two and Five (REM) sleep, with the least amount of time spent in the deep sleep of Stages Three and Four.

This process of cycling through NREM and REM sleep is something that our bodies do on their own; it happens effortlessly. Like well-oiled machines on a timer, our bodies just run. We don't have to tell our bodies how or when to sleep; they just do. We have an internal clock, called our circadian rhythm, that tells our bodies when it's time to cycle through the various sleep stages and when it's time to wake up.

Brain Signals

One of the means our bodies use to signal when it's time to sleep and time to wake up are message-carrying chemicals in

the brain called neurotransmitters. Our brains are made up of billions of nerve cells, called neurons, which communicate with each other by sending and receiving messages. These messages travel from the neuron that is sending the message (called the presynaptic neuron) over a small space between the neurons (called the synapse) to the neuron intended to receive the message (called the postsynaptic neuron). In order to cross the gap between neurons, however, the message has to be carried by a neurotransmitter.

When we're awake, certain sections of the brain produce neurotransmitters called serotonin and norepinephrine that "turn on" certain communications between neurons that keep the brain alert. Other chemicals, which "turn off" the waking signals in our brains, are released when it's time to go to sleep. According to the National Institutes of Health, certain chemicals in our blood can have a similar effect. While we are awake, a **SEDATING** chemical called adenosine is produced and progressively builds up in the bloodstream until its levels are high enough to make us drowsy, signaling that it's time to sleep. After we fall asleep, this chemical breaks down until its levels are low enough to counter the sedating effect causing us to wake up.

Sleep's chemical basis accounts for the impact certain other chemicals can have on wakefulness. Caffeine, for example, is a chemical known to stimulate the brain. It heightens the action of certain neurotransmitters, which makes the caffeine-user feel more alert. Most teens feel energized and clearer-headed after drinking a cola or cafe latte at the local coffee shop because the caffeine in these beverages impacts brain chemistry, resulting in feelings of energy and wakefulness.

If sleep and wakefulness are regulated by chemicals in our brains, you might wonder, why not just use chemicals to stay awake all the time? That might be a tempting idea, but our bod-

Many people use a cup of coffee to combat sleepiness and help them feel more alert on the job.

ies weren't designed to run without sleep. In fact, without sleep, we wouldn't survive.

What Does Sleep Do for Us?

Sufficient sleep allows us to live longer and stay healthy. Studies by the NIH on sleep deprivation in rats demonstrated just how serious an impact sleep (or lack of it) can have.

The average life span of an ordinary rat is two to three years. If you were to buy a baby rat at the pet store, and he stayed healthy, you could expect that rat to live for at least that long. Researchers tried depriving healthy rats used in a laboratory of REM sleep. Instead of living the expected two to three years, the REM-sleep-deprived rats lived only five weeks! Then scientists tried depriving other healthy rats of all five sleep stages. These rats lived only three weeks!

BLAME YOUR BODY CLOCK

Our bodies have an internal clock that runs on a twenty-four-hour cycle similar to that of time-telling clocks. This internal clock, called our circadian rhythm, creates regular, predictable patterns of wakefulness and sleep. Most people experience two periods of sleepiness: right before their longest sleep (which for most people occurs overnight) and twelve hours after mid-sleep (which for people who sleep at night would occur in early or mid-afternoon). Next time you fall asleep in your after-lunch history class, blame your circadian rhythm!

SLEEP DEPRIVATION KILLS!

In an NIH study:

average lifespan of a lab rat:
2-3-years

average lifespan of a lab rat deprived of REM sleep:
5 weeks

average lifespan of a lab rat deprived of all sleep:
3 weeks

The rats' lifespans weren't the only thing affected by lack of sleep; their immune systems were affected as well. The sleep-deprived rats developed sores on their feet and unusually low body temperatures, two symptoms that researchers accept as indicating a **COMPROMISED** immune system.

If severe sleep deprivation can cut a rat's lifespan by nearly 97 percent and compromise the animal's immune system, imagine what sleep deprivation can do to human beings!

According to most sleep researchers, sleep appears necessary (not optional) for our nervous systems to work properly. Think about the last time you were extremely tired. How clear was your thinking? How easily could you remember things? How efficiently could you add, subtract, multiply, or divide? Sufficient sleep allows our brains to work smoothly and quickly. And it also allows our bodies to work their best. Again, think about a day when you felt particularly tired. How easy was it

to run wind sprints in gym class or swim long distances? Sufficient sleep allows our minds and bodies to perform their best.

Researchers have also found that certain stages of sleep provide different benefits. Deep sleep, for example (Stages Three and Four), provides increased production of proteins (necessary for cell growth and repair of cells damaged by stress). It also fa-

cilitates the release of certain growth hormones (necessary for childhood and adolescent growth and development). REM sleep **STIMULATES** the parts of the brain used in learning.

Researchers illustrated this connection between REM sleep and learning by teaching people a new skill, allowing them to sleep for various lengths of time, then testing how much people could remember after they woke up about the skill they'd learned earlier. People who were taught a skill and allowed to sleep through all stages including REM sleep had no trouble once they woke up remembering the skill they learned earlier. People who were taught the very same skill, however, and allowed to sleep through only stages one through four but deprived of REM sleep, could not remember after they woke up the skill they'd learned earlier.

There's no doubt that sufficient sleep plays an important role in keeping our bodies and minds healthy. It helps us resist or fight off infections. It helps our bodies heal more quickly from injuries. It improves our mental abilities for accomplish-

THE BENEFITS OF SLEEP

- Sleep is necessary for survival.
- Sleep increases our resistance to disease.
- Sleep helps our immune systems work optimally.
- Sleep allows our nervous systems to work properly.
- Sleep allows neurons used during waking hours to repair themselves.
- Sleep facilitates the release of growth hormones.
- Sleep allows for greater protein production and cell repair.
- Sleep helps us function better emotionally andsocially.
- Sleep improves memory and learning abilities.

THE SKINNY ON BEAUTY SLEEP

Deep sleep is often called "beauty sleep," and maybe rightly so! During deep sleep, the body produces proteins that repair the damage done to skin by ultraviolet rays. Deep sleep truly does contribute to the beauty of healthy skin.

ing schoolwork; improves our speed, endurance, and reaction times in sports; and helps us handle stress and our emotions.

Despite the advances made in sleep research and the science of sleep, however, much is still unknown about sleep's impact on the human body. Though researchers can tell us what lack of sleep will do, they can't tell us exactly why our bodies operate the way they do. Enough is known, though, for us to realize that getting sufficient sleep is essential for our health and well-being.

Unfortunately, sufficient sleep isn't guaranteed for anyone. Even when we decide to get enough sleep, and make the choices necessary to allow for enough sleep time, we can't force ourselves to fall asleep. This is especially true if something goes wrong with the architecture, mechanics, or chemistry of our sleep.

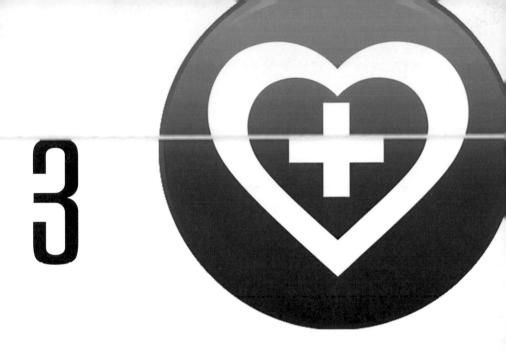

3

THE SABOTEURS OF SLEEP: What Can Go Wrong?

Anyone who has seen the movie *Sleepless in Seattle*, starring Tom Hanks and Meg Ryan, knows that the inability to sleep doesn't come only from choices we make about how we spend our time. Sometimes other issues cause us to lose sleep: grief over the loss of a loved one (as in the case of Tom Hanks' character); illness (how restful is your sleep when you have a high fever or hacking cough?); injury (imagine trying to sleep after breaking an arm, with your arm throbbing and completely immobilized in an above-the-elbow cast), noisy neighbors (ever try to sleep when the neighbors are setting off firecrackers?), a hot room (how easy is it to sleep on a hot, muggy summer night when the air conditioning is broken?), or being attacked by mosquitoes (like on that overnight camping trip you took last summer). No, sleepiness doesn't just come from choosing not to sleep enough; it can come from circumstances that can cause us to sleep less or that rob us of our quality of sleep.

Even after we realize the importance of sleep and choose to allow enough time in our schedules for adequate sleep, other things can sabotage our sleep efforts. These SABOTEURS come from four sources: environmental issues; physical issues; psychological issues; and sleep disorders.

Environmental Issues

Thirteen-year-old Scott had just about had it. This was the fifth night in a row that his newborn baby brother Ryan woke him up crying in the middle of the night. His mom and "the peanut," as Scott called Ryan, had come home from the hospital five days earlier, and as the only boy in the house, and the only child who had had a room to himself, Scott now had to share his room with his tiny sibling. His parents tried to come and get Ryan before he cried too loudly, but at least once each night since his arrival, "the peanut" had made enough noise to wake his older brother. *Baby Ryan may be a peanut in size*, Scott thought as he waited for his parents to pick up the crying infant, *but he sure makes a giant-sized noise.*

Scott's sleepiness in school the week after his newborn brother came home had nothing to do with choices he made about his time usage. He was sleepy because his baby brother wouldn't let him get a good night's sleep. The source of the teenager's sleep trouble was environmental: something about Scott's physical surroundings kept him from sleeping long or sleeping soundly.

Think about your bedroom. What makes it possible for you to sleep well at night? If you're like most teens, you need a comfy bed, sheets and blankets to keep you warm, a roof over your head to keep you dry and protected from the weather, a means to make the room dark (window blinds or curtains, for example, if a street light shines into your room at night), a few hours of silence or constant soothing sounds (like the bubbling of a fish tank), and a place where you feel relaxed and safe. All these issues—physical comfort, room temperature, room lighting, quietness, a sense of safety—are part of your environment. Your environment affects how long and how well you sleep.

If you lived in war-torn Afghanistan, for example, and heard machine gun fire or bombs going off in your neighborhood, the noise and your fear would keep you from sleeping. Or if you were homeless and slept on the street in the winter, the cold would keep you from resting soundly. Some people complain that they never sleep well in the hospital because the lights are always on, and because the intercom **SPORADICALLY** interrupts their sleep with pages for various doctors. All these issues have to do with physical surroundings, and for the most part (except in rare occasions) something can be done to change or improve sleep environments if that is the source of sleep trouble.

SOURCES OF SLEEPINESS

Sleepiness comes from two things:

1. Not enough sleep (how much we sleep).
2. Poor quality of the sleep we get (how well we sleep).

Sleep Deprivation & Its Consequences

FIFTEEN-YEAR-OLD SLEEPS FIVE YEARS!

Wouldn't that be quite a headline? In fact it's not that unusual. If we assume that most people get an average of eight hours sleep per night (which is actually less than most teens need), and there are twenty-four hours in a day, then we spend an average of one third of our lives sleeping. One third of a fifteen-year-old's life is five years.

Physical Issues

When fifteen-year-old Alex broke his leg playing soccer, he thought walking on crutches and having to take the rest of the soccer season off would be the worst of his problems. He didn't bank on not being able to sleep. Pulsing, nauseating pain and the discomfort of wearing a cast that ran from his thigh to his foot kept him from being able to rest at night. Every time he went to roll over onto his stomach—his preferred posture for sleeping—leg pain and his cast reminded him that he wouldn't be able to sleep that way. He got very little sleep until his orthopedist moved him to a below-the-knee cast weeks later.

It takes little imagination to understand how physical issues can rob us of sleep. If you've ever had a toothache, broken bone, a sore throat, bad cold, bronchitis, ear infections, severe allergies, ASTHMA, or any one of dozens of other physical conditions, you know that pain or discomfort in our bodies can keep us from getting the sleep we need. Several chronic diseases are sleep robbers as well, including JUVENILE ARTHRITIS and MUSCULAR DYSTROPHY.

WHERE YOU SLEEP AFFECTS HOW YOU SLEEP

Think about where you sleep at night, then evaluate the following factors:

COMFORT: Is your sleep spot comfortable?
SOUND: Is your sleep spot quiet or filled with soothing sounds?
CALM: Is your sleep spot away from activity?
TEMPERATURE: Is your sleep spot too hot, too cold, or just right?
LIGHTING: Is your sleep spot dark enough to encourage your body to sleep?
SECURITY: Does your sleep spot feel safe and secure?

Sometimes it's not the physical issue itself, but the medication used to treat the medical problem that is to blame. Some medicines used to treat asthma, allergies, heart problems, and other medical conditions can cause a person to have difficulty sleeping. This is called a side effect of the medication—an unintended consequence of using the drug. Insomnia, or the inability to fall asleep, is a common side effect of many medications.

Other times, the physical cause is the body's response to foods we eat or beverages we drink. Some foods contain a drug called caffeine that stimulates the brain into feeling more awake. Have you ever had a can of cola at an evening party, and then not been able to sleep when you got home? Chances are your body was reacting to the caffeine in your drink. Have you

ever eaten chocolate or some other sweet, sugary dessert late at night? Ingesting food high in sugar or chocolate content (chocolate also contains caffeine) can keep you from sleeping.

Physical habits, such as napping during the day, sleeping too long the previous night, not getting enough exercise, or exercising shortly before bedtime can also make it difficult for us to fall asleep.

These are all physical causes of sleep disruption. Sometimes, though, the trouble isn't in our bodies, but in our minds or emotions.

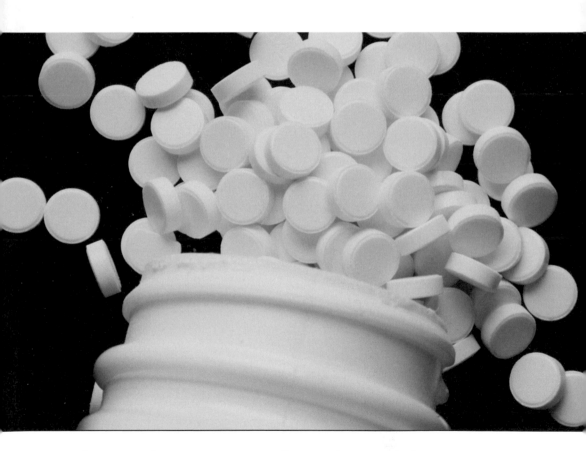

Some medications can interfere with normal sleep patterns.

If you are depressed, anxious, or angry, you may be unable to sleep.

Psychological Issues

Sixteen-year-old J.B. hoped to get into a good college, maybe even an Ivy League school, when he graduated. As a high school junior, he knew that his Scholastic Aptitude Test (SAT) scores—how well he did on the test—could make a huge difference in which schools would accept him. For weeks before his scheduled test date, he studied SAT manuals, took an SAT preparation class, studied and took practice SAT tests, and reviewed his high school math notes. He did all he could to prepare. One last thing eluded him, however: every SAT preparation manual he read emphasized getting a good night's sleep the night before the exam. J.B. tried, but no matter how hard he tried to fall asleep the Friday night before his Saturday morning exam, he just couldn't get to sleep. He was so worried about how he'd do the next morning that he spent the night lying awake while his mind raced through possible exam questions. He showed up at

CAFFEINE CHECK: HOW MUCH ARE YOU INGESTING?

8-ounce latte or capuccino at Starbucks = 75 mg. of caffeine

16-ounce Snapple iced tea = 42 mg. of caffeine

23.5-ounce Jolt beverage = 280 mg. of caffeine

12-ounce Mountain Dew = 54 mg. of caffeine

5-ounce of drip-brewed coffee = 40 to 150 mg. of caffeine

1-ounce chocolate brownie square = 6 mg. of caffeine

3 Hershey Kisses = 3 mg. of caffeine

16 ounces of chocolate milk = 8 mg. of caffeine

the exam center the next morning bleary-eyed and sleepy, despite all his preparation.

Worry, fear, anxiety, excitement—these can rob us of sleep, too. Hearing your parents argue, wondering if they'll divorce, hearing that your dad might lose his job or that your family may have to move, being excited about your first prom, looking forward to Christmas morning, getting ready for a big test, an overseas vacation, or a medical procedure can all result in stress-filled nights of little sleep. Our sleep environment and health may be fine; it's what's going on in our minds or emotions that steals our sleep away.

Sometimes these thoughts and feelings reflect normal adolescent fears and worries that pass when the crisis, situation, or source of worry is over. Other times something more—something longer lasting and more severe—is involved. These are called psychological disorders, and several psychological disorders can result in sleep disturbances: clinical depression, seasonal affective disorder (SAD), bipolar disorder (manic depression), anxiety disorders, obsessive-compulsive disorder, post-traumatic stress disorder, attention-DEFICIT/hyperactivity disorder (ADHD), and chemical addictions, to name a few.

How do you know if you have a psychological disorder? Only your doctor or a special doctor called a psychiatrist can tell you that for sure. They use a set of criteria listed in a book call the *Diagnostic and Statistical Manual of Mental Disorders* (DSM), currently in its fourth edition (DSM-IV-TR). By comparing your symptoms to specific symptoms listed for each disorder in the book, doctors can tell if you truly have a psychological disorder, and if so, which one.

If you suspect that a psychological disorder is the source of your sleep troubles, it's vital that you see your doctor or other trusted mental health professional. They can provide the help you need.

Sometimes, we can do everything right: we can allow enough time for sleep, take care of our health, provide a sleep-friendly environment, and manage our minds and emotions well, and still sleep eludes us. If that's the case, we might consider whether or not we have a sleep disorder.

Sleep Disorders

Fourteen-year-old Brady could feel his heart pounding in his chest. He felt the cold steel clench of sheer terror squeezing his throat closed. He could make no sound. His breath came in short frantic gasps as he watched the dark, hooded figures draw closer to his bedside. They'd come for him at last; there was no way out. There was nothing he could do. He desperately tried to scream, but no sound came forth. He tried to run, but his body wouldn't respond to his command. He was frozen in wide-eyed horror as he watched the beings reaching for his heart.

Then he woke up.

Brady was experiencing a common sleep problem: a nightmare. We've all had nightmares now and then, but when these sleep disturbances happen frequently, repeat themselves, or happen so often that they disrupt a person's life or cause significant distress, that person may be experiencing a nightmare disorder, one of several conditions known as sleep disorders.

When people experience sleep problems that are not caused by environmental, medical, physical, or psychological issues, they may be experiencing disturbances in their sleep architecture itself. As we've already seen, sleep can be a very complicated process. Because it's so complicated, many things can go wrong.

We can have difficulty falling asleep or staying asleep.
We can get too much of one kind of sleep and not enough of another.

We might not make it through all the stages of sleep.
We can sleep too long or have difficulty waking.
We can sleep too little and wake up too soon.
Our bodies may tell us to sleep during the day and to wake up at night.
Our bodies may tell us to sleep at the wrong times or in the wrong places.

How much we sleep (quantity) and how well we sleep (quality) work together to provide the rest our bodies need. When either of these aspects of sleep breaks down, we become sleep deprived. When that breakdown happens for no other identifiable reason (such as physical illness, environment, side effects of medication or drugs, psychological issues) doctors suspect a sleep disorder.

The American Sleep Disorders Association's *International Classification of Sleep Disorders, Diagnostic and Coding Manual* identifies seventy-eight different sleep disorders. The DSM-IV-TR, which identifies psychological disorders, simplifies the diagnostic process by categorizing primary sleep disorders into two groups: dyssomnias, which are conditions resulting from problems with the amount, quality, or timing of sleep, and parasomnias, which are characterized by unusual or abnormal behaviors that a person does while he or she is sleeping.

Some common dyssomnias, among others, include insomnia (difficulty falling asleep or staying asleep), hypersomnia (sleeping too much and having extreme difficulty waking), narcolepsy ("sleep attacks" when a person suddenly and uncontrollably falls into REM sleep during waking hours), and sleep apnea (when a person literally stops breathing for short periods of time while sleeping, then the struggle to breathe again disturbs their sleep).

Sleep Deprivation & Its Consequences

Parasomnias that many people have heard of or experienced include sleepwalking (when a person who is still asleep gets out of bed, walks around the house or leaves the house, and does simple things like talk, go to the bathroom, or open and close doors without waking), nightmares (fear episodes that occur because of bad or frightening dreams), night terrors (fear episodes unrelated to dreaming), and sleep paralysis (the inability to move when first awakening).

Though sleep disorders can contribute to the current EPI-DEMIC of sleep deprivation in North America, we won't go over these in detail in this book.

Who Cares?

"So what's the big deal?" you might ask. "What difference does it make if I don't get enough sleep, no matter what the cause? I'm not a lab rat, and I certainly won't die if I don't get enough sleep. Right?"

Maybe; maybe not.

Many teens and adults don't realize how serious sleep deprivation can be. They don't understand the toll insufficient sleep takes on bodies and minds. In the next two chapters, we'll look at the real costs of sleepiness. Then you can decide if it's worth all the fuss.

4

THE SIDE-EFFECTS OF SLEEPINESS:
How Lack of Sleep Affects School, Sports, and Physical Well-Being

It cost Molly her finger.

It cost Blake his grades.

It cost Amy her emotional stability.

It left Jared addicted to caffeine.

It cost Darnell ten days of summer camp and the confidence of being seizure-free.

Each of these teens, whose stories are told later in this chapter, lost something. They each paid a price for their lack of sleep. They didn't realize that their sleep deprivation would have consequences until it was too late.

The National Sleep Foundation study *Adolescent Sleep Needs and Patterns* identified several serious consequences of sleep deprivation in adolescents:

- increased risk of unintentional injury and death
- low grades and poor school performance
- negative moods (anger, sadness, fear, etc.)
- increased likelihood of stimulant use

Increased Risk of Unintentional Injury and Death

Seventeen-year-old Molly worked after school in a local deli making hoagies and various sandwiches for take-out orders. She'd been up late several nights in a row and had pulled an all-nighter the previous evening trying to finish up her college application essays, which she knew were due by the end of the week.

That day, after staying up all night the night before, Molly was tired. Really tired. But she had to go work. Her coworker, she knew, had called in with the flu.

In her own words, Molly tells us what happened next.

I was cleaning the meat slicer, which has a sharp, circular metal blade. The sign on the slicer says you have to be over eighteen to operate it, but at seventeen, I felt like I was close enough, so I used it all the time. Besides, my coworker had called in sick, and I had sandwiches to make. What else was I supposed to do?

To clean the slicing blade, it had to be exposed. That meant that the machine had to be turned on and the safety lifted. I'm not sure what

happened next exactly—I was so tired I could barely see straight—but I guess I wasn't paying enough attention, and while I was cleaning the front of the slicer, my finger came in contact with the spinning blade. It sliced off my right index finger right below the first joint—over an inch of my finger, right through the bone. Blood spattered everywhere. I grabbed a clean cloth to stop the bleeding and then went into shock and started screaming. Someone at the counter called 911. The ambulance came and took me and my finger, which someone had put on ice, to the ER. Doctors were able to reattach my finger, but it hasn't worked the same since.

Being tired can make us less able to cope with the demands of our days.

THE SIDE-EFFECTS OF SLEEPINESS

Tired teens can hurt themselves or others simply because they're too tired to do their jobs safely. Most teenagers work at summer jobs or part-time jobs during their junior high and high school years. The National Consumer League (NCL) estimates that 17 percent of all teens work for pay during high school. As many as five million teens may work in any given summer. But summer jobs and part-time jobs can be more dangerous than you think.

The NCL also estimates that every thirty seconds a teen worker is injured on the job and that one teen dies due to workplace injury every five days. The National Institute for Occupational Safety and Health (NIOSH) estimates that 53,000 workers under the age of eighteen are injured on the job each year and that fifty of these die due to workplace injury.

Sleep Deprivation & Its Consequences

THE UPS AND DOWNS OF TOO LITTLE SLEEP

Sleep deprivation makes these things increase (or go up):

- memory lapses
- accidents
- injuries
- mood problems
- behavior problems
- time needed to process information

Sleep deprivation makes these other things decrease (or go down)

- athletic ability (speed and endurance)
- ability to focus or concentrate
- reaction times
- alertness
- ability to learn
- ability to recall what you've learned
- quality of work or performance

Sometimes the cause of workplace injury is poor working conditions, unsafe work habits, or teens illegally being allowed to perform jobs considered unsafe for minors. Sometimes, as in Molly's case, the cause of injury is worker sleepiness.

Work isn't the only place tired teens can hurt themselves: ski slopes, weight rooms, bicycle trails, skating rinks, skate-

ALCOHOL MAKES IT WORSE

According to the NSF, sleep-deprived adolescents who consume even small amounts of alcohol are at greater risk for injury than their well-rested peers because sleep loss heightens alcohol's effects.

board parks, and even playgrounds can become dangerous for adolescents running on a shortage of sleep. Dr. Carl Hunt, of NIH's National Center on Sleep Disorders Research, noted that injuries on playground equipment are much more likely to happen when children or adolescents are sleep deprived. He summarizes his observations this way: "A tired child is an accident waiting to happen."

The National Sleep Foundation shares Dr. Hunt's concern. An Italian study reported on by the NSF, found that children under the age of fourteen who slept less than ten hours a day faced an 86 percent greater risk of accidental injury.

Low Grades and Poor School Performance

Thirteen-year-old Blake preferred the back row of seats in class. Every time his teachers allowed him and his classmates to choose their own seating, he snagged the desk in the corner of the room farthest from the teacher's desk. It's not that Blake disliked his teachers; in fact, he enjoyed most of them. It wasn't that Blake disliked school; he actually looked forward to most

of his classes. Instead, it was that Blake knew that he'd eventually nod off during class time, no matter how hard he tried to stay awake. Since his parents opened their new restaurant, he'd been working until nearly midnight almost every night of the week helping them get started until more workers could be hired. That left little time for the teenager to get the sleep he needed to function well in school. By hiding toward the back of the classroom, he hoped his teachers wouldn't notice his dozing. His hope was realized in part: his teachers didn't actually catch him sleeping in class, but they did notice the drop in his grades.

Lack of sleep can interfere with school performance.

THE SIDE-EFFECTS OF SLEEPINESS

The connection between clear thinking and adequate sleep is well documented. Grogginess, memory difficulties, and the inability to focus, pay attention, and concentrate have all been linked to unmet sleep needs. The teenager who is sleep deprived may make simple math errors, spelling mistakes, and be unable to recall as much information, which leads to lower test scores. These students may miss certain details or forget key formulas that otherwise, when rested, they wouldn't ordinarily overlook. They may even zone out in class. Dr. Mary Carskadon, the director of **CHRONOBIOLOGY** at E.P. Bradley Hospital in Rhode Island, put it this way: when tired teens show up in class their "eyes are open, but the brains are asleep." Open eyes and sleeping brains don't make for effective learning. Lack of sleep can affect school performance, as these teens can testify.

Sleepiness can cause grogginess, lack of concentration, and irritable moods.

Sleep Deprivation & Its Consequences

Negative Moods

"Just leave me alone! I don't want to talk it about it!" Amy screamed as she turned and ran up the stairs two at a time. The sound of a slamming door let Amy's mother know there would be no discussing her daughter's outburst for now.

Thirty minutes later, when her mother gently prodded, Amy's rage was explained.

"Melissa, Shannon, Kelly—they all just think of themselves," Amy explained as she started to cry. "They never think about me. I'm always the one who has to give in. I'm always the one who's the 'nice' friend. I'm always the one who has to compromise. When their boyfriends are around, they act like I don't exist, but when the guys aren't there, suddenly they want me to be with them and to do stuff with. And it's always stuff they want to do; not stuff I want to do."

"So you feel used?" Amy's mom queried gently, trying to understand.

"Yeah, I guess so. I feel like that a lot lately," the sniffling teen mumbled softly. Wiping her nose, taking a deep breath, and picking up her head, Amy seemed to get her second wind.

"And do you know what Jen did to me today?" Amy fumed through clenched teeth. "She actually had the gall to take my idea for the science brochure and use it as her own! It was my idea! It's not fair!"

Amy's mother felt her head spinning as she tried to keep track of her daughter's shifting emotions. First rage, then angry tears, then heartbreak and despair, then indignation—it was difficult to keep up.

"Do you have any idea why all this is bothering you so much right now?" Amy's mother asked softly, trying to diffuse her daughter's anger. "It's not like this is the first time these girls have done these things to you or treated you this way."

"I don't know! How am I supposed to know? It just bugs me today, that's all." Amy folded her arms and turned away.

Her mother got up to walk out of the room. Glancing at her daughter's perfectly made bed, still tidy from the day before, reminded Amy's mother that her adolescent daughter had slept very little the night before. So little, in fact, that she hadn't even bothered to crawl under the covers.

Amy's mother sighed in relief as she realized: *Amy's a basket case today because she's exhausted. Tomorrow will be a better day.*

Grumpiness, irritability, short-temperedness, and inability to control emotions have long been associated with a lack of sleep. Sleep or lack of it, remember, impacts the amount of certain neurotransmitters produced in the brain. These neurotransmitters play a huge role in the body's REGULATION of emotions. When production of these neurotransmitters is over- or under-stimulated, we can experience greater intensity of emotions and increased difficulty handling our feelings.

The NSF reports that this impact on the brain and emotions can be severe enough to trigger aggressive behaviors and depression. One study of teenage girls who stayed up later on the weekends and got less sleep found that they were more likely to experience depression than other girls the same age who did not stay up late. Another study found a direct link between shorter sleep times and behavioral problems, including aggressive behaviors in school.

Increased Likelihood of Stimulant Use

Jared had a biology exam, a geometry quiz, an oral book report presentation, and a detailed map of the Middle East all due on the same day. He'd been working on the book report and map for nearly two weeks, but the bio exam and math quiz caught him by surprise.

How am I going to get all this done? The fifteen-year-old stared at the work spread out on his desk. *I'm never going to finish.*

Jared knew that his only alternative was to stay up late. But it was almost eleven o'clock, and he was fading fast. *A cappuccino will do the trick.*

He grabbed his jacket from the back of his chair, trotted downstairs, and out the front door. The local doughnut shop across the street from his house was open twenty-four hours a day, and it sold some really good cappuccino.

Unfortunately for Jared, his near-midnight cappuccino runs became an almost-nightly routine, and by the end of the school year, he was addicted to caffeine.

Teenagers—like everyone else—need adequate sleep in order to concentrate.

Diminished sleep times can create a number of problems, both emotional and physical.

Sleep Deprivation & Its Consequences

COMMON BRAND NAMES OF CAFFEINE PRODUCTS

- NoDoz
- Pep-Back or Ultra Pep-Back
- Quick-Pep
- Enerjets
- SnapBack (by prescription only)
- Cafcit (by prescription only)
- Dexitac Stay Alert Stimulant
- Caffedrine (by prescription only)
- Vivarin

What do you do when, like Jared, you have a lot of work that has to get done, yet feel too sleepy to do it? If you're like many teens, you reach for a caffeine-laced beverage like Jolt, Coke, Pepsi, or Mountain Dew. If a soda isn't handy, you might take a caffeine-loaded caplet.

How about when you wake up in the morning feeling too tired to face the day? Many teens grab a cup of designer coffee not because they like coffee for its taste, but because of the energy boost it provides. Some tired teens reach for other pick-me-ups, including cigarettes or illegal drugs.

All of these substances are stimulants: they are chemicals that have a stimulating effect on the brain and its chemistry. Stimulants, whether caffeine or nicotine or any of the others, provide a short-term boost of energy and alertness. The "kick" they provide also prevents sleep.

Stimulant use can lead to a vicious cycle of sleeplessness. A sleep-deprived teenager drinks coffee to help herself feel more energetic and alert, but the same coffee that helps her get through the day keeps her up at night, preventing her from getting the sleep she needs to feel rested. She wakes up the next day, just as tired as she was before, so she drinks more coffee. The coffee again helps her stay alert during waking hours, but also keeps her up at night again. The teen still doesn't get much sleep, so she wakes up exhausted again. She grabs more coffee, and the cycle continues, seemingly without end.

Often complicating this cycle is a growing chemical dependence on caffeine. The brain gets used to having caffeine to stimulate its production of neurotransmitters, so it adjusts its own chemistry to include regular shots of caffeine. If someone like Jared tries to stop drinking caffeinated beverages after his body has grown dependent on them, he will experience several unpleasant physical symptoms, the worst of which is often a severe headache, but which can also include the jitters, irritability, inability to sleep, and many more. When a person experiences these symptoms, he is said to be experiencing caffeine withdrawal.

In addition to the four consequences of sleep-deprivation in adolescents identified by the NSF and discussed so far in this chapter, inadequate sleep can affect overall health and physical stamina.

Physical Well-Being

"Hi, Mom," was the first thing Darnell could think of to say when he heard his mother's voice on his cell phone.

"Darnell, is that you?" his mom asked in surprise. "Is everything all right? Normally they don't let you call from camp, do they?"

Stimulants like caffeine may make you feel more awake—but they cannot give your body the energy it needs to exercise.

Darnell was only four days into his two-week adventure camp, and the fact that he had called home meant something must be wrong.

Darnell paused.

"I had a seizure."

"You what? Aw, sweetie. I'm sorry. Are you okay?"

"Yeah. It was only a mild one this time, and the camp nurse gave me an extra dose of my seizure meds, but they think I'd better come home, just in case."

Seizures were nothing new to Darnell or his mom. He'd had a **SEIZURE DISORDER** since he was little, and had long been on medications that prevented him from seizing again. The fifteen-year-old hadn't had a full-blown seizure in more than three years.

"What do you think happened?" Darnell's mother asked gently. "Do you have any idea? I mean, it's been so long, and the **NEUROLOGIST** said your medication levels were right where they should be. Do you think this medication isn't working anymore?"

"No, I think the medicine's fine."

"Then what do you think happened?"

"Well," Darnell sighed, "the guys in my cabin are really rowdy, you know, like wise guys and class clowns. And they tend to ignore the lights out stuff and pull stupid pranks. Last night they were messing around until after 4:00 a.m. I haven't gotten much sleep in the last four days."

"Why didn't you say something?"

"I just want to be one of the guys, Mom. I don't want to be the kid with **EPILEPSY**. I just want to fit in. Everyone else shouldn't have to go to sleep at night on account of me."

"But you know sleep makes a huge difference in your seizures."

"Yeah, I know, but I thought just this once it would be okay."

"I guess it wasn't, huh?"

"Guess not."

Sleep and physical well-being are closely connected.

THE SIDE-EFFECTS OF SLEEPINESS

"So what do you want to do?"

"Camp director thinks I need to go home. I suppose I should. Can you drive up and get me?"

"Sure, Bud. Your Dad and I will be there by mid-afternoon."

Sleep deprivation can affect a teenager's physical health in several ways. We saw in chapter 2 that sleep deprivation could reduce the immune system's ability to fight off infection and disease. According to a study cited in *Science News*, one night's loss of sleep can reduce the number of infection-fighting immune cells in your blood by as much as 30 percent. Fewer immune cells means less ability to resist colds, flus, and other common illnesses. Teens who chronically get less sleep than they need often end up with **RECURRENT** colds or other illnesses. In Darnell's case, his wasn't a chronic or recurrent illness that was impacted by his lack of sleep, but a chronic, permanent condition called a seizure disorder, also commonly referred to as epilepsy.

Researchers have established a link between sleep deprivation and increased incidences of seizures in those with existing seizure disorders. Seizures occur when the brain's electrical signaling goes haywire or out of control. Simply put, seizures could be described as an overload of electrical activity in the brain. Imagine, if you will, that a person with a seizure disorder has an invisible containment field in his brain, called a threshold. Medications keep the containment field, or threshold, at a strength sufficient to keep the electrical activity contained and to allow the person to function normally yet remain seizure-free. When the threshold is lowered or weakened, electrical activity can break through so that it's no longer contained, and the person can have a seizure. Many things can lower or weaken seizure thresholds: not enough anti-seizure medication, drugs or alcohol, and not enough sleep.

As you can see from the consequences we've looked at in this chapter, sleep deprivation is serious business. Too little sleep can take its toll. As Dr. Mary Carskadon, Director of Sleep Research at Bradley Hospital summarizes in an interview with CNN, "Kids are too sleepy to learn well. They're too sleepy to be happy. And they're at great risk for such things as traffic accidents."

5

DROWSY DRIVING:
The Unexpected Killer

A van driver, after being up for thirty hours straight, fell asleep while driving and killed a twenty-year-old college student.

The student named "America's Safest Teen Driver" in 1990 fell asleep behind the wheel of his car late one afternoon, killing both himself and the teen driver of the oncoming vehicle with which he collided.

A high school track star driving home from a state track meet fell asleep behind the wheel of her car just moments before arriving home. She died in the ensuing accident.

Drowsy driving will cause over 100,000 motor vehicle accidents this year.

An eighteen-year-old high school graduate on his way home from work dozed off as he drove and didn't notice his car drifting toward the edge of the highway. At the same time and place, a forty-six-year-old husband and father was on the side of the road helping two young women change their flat tire. The dozing teen's car hit and killed the man.

Each of these is a true event taken from news story headlines. Magazines, newspapers, online reports, and television programs are filled with such stories nearly every day. When talking about sleepiness, motor vehicle accidents, injuries, and fatalities are the most serious and most deadly consequence of sleep deprivation.

Consider these findings from a 2005 study conducted by the National Sleep Foundation: an estimated 60 percent of adult drivers have driven while drowsy in the past year and more than 37 percent (more than 100 million people) say they've fallen asleep while driving. More than 12 percent say they fall asleep at the wheel at least once each month.

"Yeah, but those surveys are about old people," you might object. "They don't really apply to teens." Not true, according to the National Sleep Foundation. Drivers between eighteen and twenty-nine are much more likely to be involved in a sleep-related crash than those over age thirty. Another study found that twenty years was the peak age for drowsy-driving accidents and that young people (defined as being between sixteen and twenty years of age) were the single age group most likely to be involved in a fall-asleep crash. A third study concluded that eighteen- to twenty-four-year olds were over-represented in crashes involving sleep.

Other National Sleep Foundation findings confirm how widespread and costly the problem of drowsy driving really is. We learned earlier that falling asleep while driving is responsible for at least 100,000 automobile crashes, 71,000 injuries, 1,550 fatalities, and $12.5 billion in property damage and lost work time each year. The crashes cited in these statistics usually occurred between 4:00 and 6:00 a.m., and involved sober drivers in single vehicles traveling alone whose cars left the roadway without their making any attempt to avoid the crash (the drivers didn't brake, slow down, or counter steer). Most experts think these numbers are low since these figures don't include crashes that happened during daytime hours, involved multiple vehicles, or included driver attempts to avoid the crash.

The NHTSA estimates that driver inattention causes an additional one million crashes annually. With the connection between sleep deprivation and inability to focus so well established, it is thought that many of these accidents are related to sleepiness as well.

Drowsy driving is becoming a national epidemic, according to some experts, even more problematic and more common than drunk driving.

"Fall-asleep car crashes probably kill more Americans under the age of twenty-five than alcohol-related accidents," said sleep expert Dr. Mark Mahowald in an interview with CBS news correspondent Bob McNamara. A study done by Minnesota health and safety agencies illustrated Mahowald's point.

WHO IS MOST AT RISK?

Though any driver can fall asleep at the wheel, the NHTSA has identified three groups as those most likely to be involved in drowsy driving incidents:

- young people aged sixteen to twenty-nine
- shift workers who work at night or who work long or irregular hours
- people with untreated sleep disorders

The agencies recruited two college students to participate in driving evaluations. The first evaluation was done after allowing the students to have several consecutive nights of regular sleep. After a week of normal sleep, both students drove well and reacted appropriately and safely to simulated road hazards and weather conditions.

After taking the first driving test, the students were not allowed to sleep for the next twenty-fours. Then they were tested again. After being awake all night, like many students might be when cramming for final exams or working on big projects or presentations, both students performed poorly in the second driving test. One of them even fell asleep at the wheel, stopped steering, and failed to stop. When interviewed after the test, the student said she didn't even remember she was driving.

Summarizing the student's driving test results, Dr. Mahowald said, "They were as impaired behind the wheel as if they had a blood alcohol level of point-one percent." In all states, 0.1 percent blood alcohol content is considered legally intoxicated. In other countries, especially European nations, and in some states it's even less.

NOT MUCH DIFFERENCE BETWEEN DROWSY AND DRUNK

The *New York Times* reports that when tested on a driving simulator and when given eye-hand coordination tasks to do, people who had been sleep deprived did just as poorly as those who were legally drunk.

Sleep researchers and traffic safety specialists now concur: driving drowsy is every bit, if not more, dangerous than driving drunk.

What Happens to the Drowsy Driver?

Courtney was an honors student who lived on a farm in a rural area far away from any "real" towns (as she called them). Her college placement exams were being held in a small city about an hour away. After staying up most of the night going over practice problems, the sixteen-year-old drove the forty-five miles of four-lane highway to the testing center without incident. After taking the three-hour test, Courtney drove to a nearby fast-food restaurant, ordered lunch to go, and started her journey home.

About thirty minutes into her trip, the high-school junior realized she didn't know how far she'd traveled on the highway, and she didn't remember driving for the past few minutes. Ten minutes later, the sound of the rumble strips along the highway's shoulder startled her into alertness. The rumble strips may have saved the teenager's life.

The highway is a dangerous place to be sleepy!

DROWSY DRIVING: The Unexpected Killer

Lack of sleep can make dangerous road conditions even more challenging to maneuver.

Sleep Deprivation & Its Consequences

Courtney's experience is typical of most drowsy-driving incidents. Research done by the Federal Highway Administration shows that the most common automobile accident nationwide is the single-vehicle-that-runs-off-the-road crash—the crash most often associated with drowsy driving. These accidents account for 64.4 percent of all single-vehicle crashes. The Pennsylvania Turnpike Commission and New York State Thruway officials estimate that drowsy drivers cause nearly 50 percent of fatal crashes on their states' highways.

Driving over long stretches of boring highway can have a hypnotic effect on any driver. The drowsy driver is even more susceptible to these sleep-inducing effects. What are some of the things that signal you're becoming too drowsy to drive? Like Courtney, sometimes the first symptom is that you can't remember the last few miles driven. You zoned out. Other symptoms include:

- drifting in your lane
- driving on the rumble strip
- crossing the center line or grazing the median
- daydreaming
- yawning over and over again
- having difficulty keeping your eyes open
- missing traffic signs or exits
- having trouble sitting up straight
- over steering to make a driving correction (swerving too sharply, braking too hard, etc.)

If you experience these symptoms while driving, or if someone you're riding with does, pull the car over immediately. It might save your life.

You Can't Control When You Fall Asleep

The reason it's so important to stop driving when you're drowsy is because you cannot predict or control when you will fall asleep. In a study done by the NSF, four out of five sleep-deprived subjects failed to predict when they would nod off. Most fell asleep before making the prediction.

If you recall, the first stage of sleep is that drowsy stage where you are still vaguely aware of your surroundings. Most people deny even being asleep if awakened from this stage. They don't even realize they've been dozing. The same thing is true of drowsy drivers. Most don't know they've drifted into sleep until the blare of another car horn or the loud thumping of a rumble strip alerts them to their slumber. That's what happened to Gabrielle.

"Don't worry about me, Mom," Gabrielle assured her mother as she kissed her goodbye. "I can tell when I'm getting too sleepy to drive. If I start to get too tired or think I might fall asleep, I'll stop at a rest stop. Don't worry; I won't let myself doze off. Love you! I'll call you when I get to school." These were Gabrielle's last words to her family.

She thought she could handle the drive from just outside her home near Philadelphia to her college home-away-from-home in central Michigan. Anxious to get back to school after a busy spring break, the nineteen-year-old college sophomore loaded up her '91 Ford Explorer and started the twelve-hour drive.

Gabrielle was alert and responsive as she made her way down the Northeast Extension of Route 476 to Pennsylvania's East-West Turnpike early that Sunday morning. With little traffic, driving was a breeze. Two hours later, she crossed the Susquehanna River and entered a long, lonely stretch of highway through state game lands. Passing through tunnels near

Long straight stretches of highway can be as dangerous as curves and hills, since the monotonous road can lull you into sleepiness.

Drowsy Driving: The Unexpected Killer

the Allegheny Mountains broke up the tedium of the first part of her drive, but the teenager soon found herself yawning and daydreaming.

She cranked the radio, rolled down the window, and took a sip of the Diet Coke she'd brought along. That helped for just a few minutes, but not enough to save her.

Anyone driving across Pennsylvania knows it can be a long drive and dangerous, too. After driving long stretches of boring highway through central parts of the state, the PA Turnpike becomes a winding path through the mountains further west—it's a terrible stretch of highway for drowsy drivers who don't anticipate its dangers.

Around 1:30 p.m., about five hours after beginning her trek, the humming road beneath her wheels increased its hypnotic effect. Who knows what Gabrielle was thinking about when she entered that stretch of highway? Maybe she was recalling the laughter she'd shared with old friends late into the wee hours

DROWSY DRIVING ACCIDENT PROFILE

Sleep-related crashes have these characteristics:

- usually occur late at night or mid afternoon
- often result in serious injury or death
- usually result from a single vehicle going off the road
- usually occur on a high-speed highway
- driver usually does nothing to avoid the accident (no skid marks, etc.)
- driver is usually alone in the car

THE CAUSES OF DROWSY DRIVING

Any one of the following can cause sleepiness behind the wheel:

- alcohol
- some medications
- some illnesses or medical conditions
- not sleeping enough
- not sleeping well
- getting only sporadic, fragmented sleep
- working jobs that restrict sleep or that change sleep/wake cycles

of that morning; maybe she was running through her outline for the mid-term paper due the following the week. Maybe her mind had wandered to the Middle East where her Marine brother had recently been deployed. No one can know for sure.

Just east of the turnpike's New Stanton exit, the four-lane divided highway develops some dangerously sharp curves and inclines. This part of the highway becomes narrower, too, as it closes in on the suburbs surrounding Pittsburgh. Gabrielle found herself in the left of two westbound lanes as she slowly passed an eighteen-wheeler. As she passed the slower moving vehicle, the road curved to the right as it went up a slight rise. It was here that investigators believe Gabrielle dozed off.

Instead of following the curve to the right, the college-bound student's car kept going straight and grazed the highway's center concrete divider. The sudden scraping startled Gabrielle, who immediately woke up and realized that she had started to run off the road. To get back on, she over-steered, jerking the steering wheel back to the right, which sent her car careening back over the two westbound lanes, right in front of the truck she'd just passed, and head on into the guardrails. In the space of less than two seconds, Gabrielle's vehicle had gone from seventy miles per hour to a complete stop.

The force of the crash pinned Gabrielle in her SUV, which miraculously had not rolled. She couldn't feel her feet, she told the first people on the scene. Paramedics told her that her pelvis was crushed, her legs were broken, and that she probably had internal injuries. As they waited for the Medivac chopper to arrive, the paramedics watched Gabrielle fall in and out of consciousness. By the time the emergency chopper got to the scene, she was dead.

One false belief—that she could control when she fell asleep—cost this teen her life. It was a deadly mistake.

The best way to avoid drowsy driving is to avoid sleep deprivation, and the best way to avoid sleep deprivation is to get

DROWSY DRIVING COULD PUT YOU IN JAIL

In 2003, the first law was passed in the United States making it a crime to knowingly drive drowsy. Thanks to New Jersey's "Maggie's Law," if you're a driver involved in a car accident in that state, and the accident kills someone, and you went without sleep for the twenty-four hours preceding the crash yet chose to drive anyway, the police can charge you with vehicular homicide, which can get you up to ten years in prison and a $150,000 fine.

Sleep Deprivation & Its Consequences

FIVE FACTS THAT COULD SAVE YOUR LIFE

FACT ONE: Rolling down a window or listening to music while driving will not keep you from falling asleep at the wheel if you're drowsy.

FACT TWO: If you are sleep-deprived, one beer can have the same impact on you that two or three beers would have if you were well rested.

FACT THREE: Getting a good night's sleep before a long drive can mean the difference between having a safe journey and having one that kills you.

FACT FOUR: Drinking coffee or caffeinated soda may help you stay awake for short times, but after your caffeine high you can become even more sleepy.

FACT FIVE: The only proven way to wake yourself up if you're sleepy while driving is to pull over and take a fifteen- or twenty-minute nap.

enough sleep. You may not be able to control when you fall asleep, but you have much to say about how much sleep you get.

Don't Be the Next Statistic

The good news is that drowsy driving is an avoidable condition. You don't have to drive while you're sleepy. Try these tips, provided in full by the NSF, to help make your next driving experience a safer one:

DROWSY DRIVING: The Unexpected Killer

"Crash in bed, not on the road!"

"When you're short on sleep, stay out of the driver's seat."

—Claude Lenfant, M.D. Director, National Heart, Lung, and Blood Institute

1. Start any trip by getting enough sleep the night before. Plan to drive during the times of day when you are normally awake, and stay overnight rather than traveling straight through.
2. Avoid driving during your body's "down time." Take a mid-afternoon break and find a place to sleep between midnight and 6 a.m.
3. Talk with your passenger if you have someone else in the car. A passenger can also let you know when you are showing signs of sleepiness. If your passenger thinks you are getting sleepy, let someone else drive or pull over and sleep. A nap could save your life and the lives of others.
4. Make sure both people in the front of the car are awake. A driver who needs rest should go to the back seat, buckle up, and sleep.
5. Schedule a break every two hours or every one hundred miles. Stop sooner if you show any danger signs of sleepiness. When you stop for your break take a nap, stretch, take a walk, and get some exercise before getting back into the car.

Other things to remember that can save your life or the lives of your friends and loved ones: don't let friends drive drowsy; refuse to ride with a driver you know is drowsy or sleep deprived; if you know you haven't had enough sleep let someone else do the driving; don't drive alone or with a sleeping passenger—make sure you have someone in the passenger seat who is awake; don't drive if you're on medications that can make you sleepy; and don't drive even short distances if you're seriously sleep deprived.

6

SELF-HELP FOR SLEEPINESS:
Tips for Getting a
Good Night's Sleep

D o you think you know all you need to know about sleep
deprivation and its consequences for adolescents? Take a
quick quiz to find out. Which of the following statements
are true, and which are false?

1. Teens need less sleep than their younger siblings.
2. All sleep is the same.

3. Quality of sleep doesn't matter; it's just how much sleep you get.
4. If you don't get enough sleep during the week, you can make up for it on the weekends.
5. Consuming caffeine refreshes you as well as sleep does.
6. Lack of sleep affects only physical abilities; not mental abilities.
7. People who sleep less are healthier.
8. Everyone should get eight hours of sleep.
9. Driving under the influence of alcohol or drugs is far more dangerous than driving drowsy.
10. Cranking the stereo, munching on snacks, and rolling the window down will keep you awake when you drive.

How many do you think are true? How many are false? If you read the earlier chapters of this book carefully, you would know that every one of these statements is false. As we saw in the previous chapter, holding false ideas about sleep can cost you your life.

The Truth About Sleep and Sleepiness

So what's the bottom line on sleep? Adequate sleep is a biological need essential for our health, safety, and emotional well-being. Without enough sleep, something or someone gets hurt. When we regularly don't get the amount or quality of sleep we need, we end up sleep deprived, which can make us chronically drowsy. This chronic sleepiness can have disastrous, even fatal consequences.

Sleepy or Tired?

Before discussing how to reduce our sleepiness, we need to realize that sleepiness is not the opposite of being energetic, nor is it the same thing as being tired or fatigued. Tiredness and fatigue are conditions where the body feels weaker or worn out after exertion or because of illness. After a hard workout, for example, you may be tired, but you probably won't be sleepy.

Sleepiness is the condition where your body has a nearly irresistible urge to fall asleep. You may or may not be fatigued, but you desperately want to sleep.

Sleep deprivation can lead to both fatigue and sleepiness, but sleepiness (also called drowsiness) causes the more dangerous consequences.

To combat sleepiness, we need to combat sleep deprivation, and the best antidote to sleep deprivation, as we saw in earlier chapters, is getting enough sleep.

Getting the Rest We Need

Bobby has a terrible time waking up in the morning. He feels like his head doesn't even clear until after lunch. He really gets

THE NATIONAL HEART, LUNG, AND BLOOD INSTITUTE'S TOP FIVE REASONS TO GET ENOUGH SLEEP

1. Drowsy drivers crash their cars.
2. Drowsy teens react more slowly and perform worse in sports.
3. Drowsy teens do poorly in school and have problems socially.
4. Drowsy teens have trouble making good decisions.
5. Drowsy teens don't look their best.

If you're sleep deprived you won't need to count sheep to fall asleep—the urge may be irresistible!

Sleep Deprivation & Its Consequences

rolling after dinner and is raring to go by 11:00 p.m. Some people would call Bobby a night owl.

Charnelle is just the opposite. Even as a teenager, she prefers the early hours of the day. First period classes are always her best because that's the time of day during which she feels most awake. Some people might call her an early riser.

Brittany seems to be able to stay up late or get up early. It doesn't really matter to her. The main thing, as far as Britt is concerned, is that she squeezes in her nine hours of sleep. Then she's up for just about anything.

None of these teens is doing anything wrong. They're body clocks just run according to different patterns. Bobby's internal rhythm makes him more alert later in the day and sleepier earlier in the morning. Charnelle's is just the opposite. Brittany's seems to be flexible. As these teens illustrate, not everyone needs the same amount of sleep, nor does everyone need to sleep at the same time. To tell these teens that their sleep architecture has to follow one, best-for-everybody cycle would be just as silly as saying they have the same hair color or height. Every teen is unique and has a sleep-wake cycle all her own.

When considering how much sleep is healthiest, you have to decide not only how much sleep is best for you, but what time of day is best for you to sleep. Ask yourself these questions:

1. When I'm getting enough regular sleep, what times of the day do I feel most alert?
2. What times are my "slump" times or when do I feel least energetic.
3. At what time of day do I pay attention best?
4. At what time of day do I fall asleep the easiest?
5. How much sleep do I need to get to consistently wake up feeling refreshed?

Sleep Deprivation & Its Consequences

6. If I didn't set an alarm, and went to bed at a reasonable hour, what time would I wake up?

7. How long does it take me to fall asleep at night after I go to bed?

Your answers to these questions will help you identify the best sleep patterns for you. Remember, the one sure-fire sign that you're well rested is if you wake up feeling alert and refreshed.

Different Problems, Different Solutions

We saw in chapters 1 and 2 that sleep deprivation can be caused by several things: lifestyle choices, how we spend our time, environmental issues, physical issues, psychological issues, and sleep disorders. While this book can't address solutions for every one of these robbers of sleep, here are a few tips to get you started.

Solutions for Sleep Deprivation
Caused by Lifestyle and Time Usage

Do you remember Sarah whose episode of oversleeping started this book? Sarah's chronic sleep deprivation resulted from specific choices she made about her life and schedule. She chose to hold a part-time job. She chose to do lengthy workouts at the gym each morning. She chose to have a pet. She chose to invest time in outings with friends on school nights. Sarah didn't have to do any of those things. Yes, she had to attend school; she had to eat; she had to shower (activities necessary for personal hygiene are non-negotiable when you're thinking about how to use your time); and you could even say she had to do her homework (well, only if she wanted to get good grades and get into

FIVE TIPS TO HELP YOU MANAGE YOUR TIME

1. Make a list of things you want to do, but don't seem to have time for. When you're bored or find yourself wasting time, do something on the list.
2. Set time limits for certain activities (cleaning house, doing homework, watching TV, playing video games, chatting on the computer, etc.).
3. Keep as much routine in your day as possible.
4. Make a schedule of your day to see where your time goes.
5. Use a date book or calendar to plan your work and activities.

college). Her day was a blend of things she wanted to do and things she had to do.

Are exercising regularly, caring for pets, taking a part-time job, and hanging out with friends good things? You bet they are. Are they needed? Sometimes. Sarah's problem was that she felt like she had to do them all, all the time.

If you remember anything at all from this book, remember two things:

1. Sleep deprivation can kill you.
2. Sometimes you have to say "no" to very good things in order to say "yes" to the best.

Our lifestyle choices rarely involve choosing between two really bad things. More often than not we have to choose between equally VALID options. That's where determining what is essential is important.

What things in your life are so important that you couldn't live or stay healthy without them? You have to eat. You have to drink. You have to bathe and have clean clothes. Exercise, in moderation, is also essential for health, as is time with friends. Every bit as important as all of these things is sleep.

To get a handle on your lifestyle choices try this exercise. Divide a sheet of paper into three rows and three columns. Label the rows: "Musts/Needs," "Wants/Desires," and "Everything Else." Next, create the columns, labeling one "activity" and the other "time needed." You've just created a time-use chart. Your blank chart might look something like this:

Once you have your chart made, write down all the things that are necessary for your health and survival in the first row, and how much time (in hours) those things take. This list will include eating, sleeping, personal hygiene, any necessary medical routines, and so on. Also in the first row, write down anything

	Activity	Time Needed
MUSTS/ NEEDS		
WANTS/ DESIRES		
EVERYTHING ELSE		

that is required of you that must get done: things like going to school, taking care of a pet, family chores, or attending family events, and note how much time you invest in these. In the second row, write down all that you want to do and how much time is involved. That might include school activities, outings with friends, music lessons, multiple sports, hobbies, watching TV, talking on the phone, surfing the Internet, and just about anything else that's important to you. Row two is for things you really want to do. In the third row, write down anything else you're involved in that isn't in row one or two.

Now total the number of hours listed in each row. Remember, one week has only 168 hours; you can't use more than that.

How does your chart look? Do you have too many hours in rows two and three, and not enough in row one? Are you over 168 hours?

The activities listed in row one should be non-negotiable. Don't forget to include nine hours of sleep per night, or sixty-three hours for sleep in that row. If you have to "squeeze" anything in, it shouldn't be sleep; it should be an activity from rows two or three.

Sometimes seeing our activities and lifestyle choices on paper can help us discover where we can make time for more sleep. Another way to approach lifestyle issues is to ask, "What can I give up in order to get more sleep?" Here, too, the idea of needs versus wants comes into play. "Do I really need this job, or do I just like the extra money?" "Do I really need to do two sports each season, or can I settle for just one?" If getting enough sleep was mandated by law and not getting enough sleep was punishable by death, what would you give up in order to stay off death row?

Sometimes we end up with sleep-depriving lifestyles because we've never taken the time to be deliberate about what we do. If lifestyle issues are robbing you of necessary sleep, take

Sleep Deprivation & Its Consequences

some time to see where you're spending time that could otherwise be used for lifesaving sleep. Being more deliberate about ~~the use of your time can free up time for sleep from many un~~ expected places.

Solutions for Environment-Caused Sleep Deprivation

As we stated earlier, sleep problems caused by environmental issues are the easiest to correct. If you have a TV in your room that keeps you from getting the sleep you need, move the TV to another place in your house. If your prowling cat wakes you up by pouncing on your bed in the middle of the night, close the feline off in a separate room away from you overnight. If your bedroom is cold, stock up on extra blankets. If your bedroom is too hot, invest in a fan or air conditioner. If your brother snores, get a good pair of earplugs or ask if you can sleep in a different place in the house. If a fish tank light keeps you awake, but your roommate insists that it be on, buy an inexpensive sleep mask to cover your eyes (available at your local drug store).

Most environmental issues (except crime, war, abusive home environments, or proximity to flight paths or railways, for example) can be solved with just a bit of creative thinking.

Solutions for Physical Problems Causing Sleep Loss

Josh regularly had a double dip serving of Rocky Road ice cream for a bedtime snack. He also took an unusually long time to fall asleep. Sharon, who worked the evening shift at an all-night coffee shop, had the same problem, only her midnight munchies in-

Sleep issues can be caused by stress, as well as environmental disturbances.

Sleep Deprivation & Its Consequences

TRY THIS!

For two days, keep a diary of everything you do and how long you do it (that means everything). You may be surprised by where you spend your time.

cluded café latte and home-baked chocolate-chip cookies. Both suffered sleep deprivation because of their bodies' responses to sugar and caffeine.

Dietary issues that cause sleep problems, like environmental issues, are easy to address. You just have to be willing. Two of the most common suggestions made by sleep professionals for improving the quality of your sleep are to avoid caffeine at least six hours before bedtime and to avoid sweets after dinner. These two small changes can make an enormous difference in your ability to fall asleep at night.

If you must munch at night, trade high sugar or high carbohydrate foods for foods rich in potassium or calcium: bananas, yogurt, and warm milk are all known to have sleep-causing qualities.

Health issues are far more difficult to solve. Thankfully, many health-rooted sleep disruptions are short-lived. Colds, coughs, seasonal allergies, broken bones, and other temporary conditions last only a few weeks at a time. For the most part, you can put up with the temporary sleep loss. But if need be, your doctor can prescribe a short-term medication that will help you sleep. This is often unnecessary, however, because many medicines used to treat allergies, colds, and other short-term conditions have sedating (sleep-inducing) effects.

A hot bath can help you relax.

Sleep Deprivation & Its Consequences

FIND TIME NOW!

Need time to sleep? Try these instant time finders:

- Turn off the TV.
- Cut your Instant Messaging and cell phone chat time in half.
- Play one less video or computer game per day.

Other health conditions are more difficult to address and should be discussed with your doctor. If it's not the health condition itself, but the medication used to treat the condition that's robbing you of much-needed z's, you should talk with your doctor about this, too. She may be able to switch to a different, just as effective drug treatment.

FIVE RELAXING ACTIVITIES YOU CAN DO BEFORE BEDTIME

1. Take a hot soak in the bathtub.
2. Have someone massage your neck and back muscles.
3. Meditate or pray.
4. Read.
5. Listen to soft, soothing music.

Many cold medications can cause sleepiness. Be careful what you are taking, though—check expiration dates and discard old medicines.

Solutions for Psychological Problems or Sleep Disorders Causing Inadequate Sleep

Dan fumed when he walked through the door from work at ten o'clock Friday evening. As a cashier at a local grocery story, his job was usually pretty low-key and low-stress. But someone in accounting had made an error during his shift and told him his cash drawer was $300 short. The store manager accused him of stealing the money. The seventeen-year-old high school senior's conscience was clear; he knew he hadn't taken the money. But he was peeved that he'd been falsely accused.

While trying to fall asleep that night, he replayed the conversation he'd had with his manager over and over again in his mind. With every instant replay, he grew more tense and angry. Any thought of sleep crept further away the more he mulled over his fate.

Dan's inability to sleep stemmed directly from his thoughts and emotions. What could he have done to have gotten more sleep?

He could have taken a long, hot shower to help his muscles relax. He could have put on soothing music or listened to a radio talk show. He could have chosen not to think about what happened at work, and focused on something else instead—by reading a book or doing an easy crossword puzzle, for example. He could have vented his frustration on paper or in a conversation with a friend, and then done any quiet activity that helped him relax, like listening to his CDs, playing his guitar, or building a model. He could have meditated or prayed.

Any of these activities can help you fall asleep faster when you feel stressed or angry. When emotional or psychological barriers to sleep are rooted in psychiatric disorders, however, many of the actions suggested for Dan may not work. These need to be discussed with a psychiatrist, family physician, or

Sleep Deprivation & Its Consequences

THE NATIONAL SLEEP FOUNDATION'S TOP TEN SLEEP TIPS

1. Keep a regular sleep schedule.
2. Avoid caffeine.
3. Avoid nicotine.
4. Avoid alcohol.
5. Don't eat or drink too much close to bedtime.
6. Exercise (at the right time) promotes sleep.
7. Use relaxing bedtime rituals.
8. Create a sleep-promoting environment.
9. Associate your bed with sleep only.
10. Sleep on a comfortable mattress and pillows.

other health professional. The same could be said for diagnosed sleep disorders. We won't attempt to provide solutions for these issues here.

Sleep. It provides food for the brain, rest for the body, and rejuvenates the soul. With it, we function our best and stay healthiest. Without it, we function poorly and put ourselves at risk for illness, injury, even death.

Do you feel sleep-deprived? Chances are there is something you can do right now, right here, today, to improve the amount and quality of the sleep your body so desperately needs. Will you choose sleep-deprivation and its consequences, or will you choose the health and well-being only adequate sleep habits can bring? The choice is up to you.

Further Reading

Bayer, Linda. *Sleep Disorders*. Philadelphia: Chelsea House, 2001.

Dement, M.D., Ph.D., William C. *The Promise of Sleep: A Pioneer in Sleep Medicine Explores the Vital Connection Between Health, Happiness, and a Good Night's Sleep*. New York: Dell, 2000.

Drummond, Dr. Edward. *The Complete Guide to Psychiatric Drugs: Straight Talk for Best Results*. New York: John Wiley and Sons, 2000.

Esherick, Joan. *Sleep Disorders and Their Treatment*. Philadelphia, Penn.: Mason Crest, 2004.

Hirschkowitz, Max and Patricia B. Smith. *Sleep Disorders for Dummies*. Hoboken, N.J.: Wiley, 2004.

Wilens, Timothy. *Straight Talk about Psychiatric Medications for Kids*. New York: The Guilford Press, 2001.

For More Information

AAA Foundation For Traffic Safety
www.aaafoundation.org/home

American Academy of Sleep Medicine
www.aasmnet.org

American Sleep Apnea Association
www.sleepapnea.org

Better Sleep Council
www.bettersleep.org

Narcolepsy Network
www.narcolepsynetwork.org

National Center on Sleep Disorders Research
National Heart, Lung, and Blood Institute
www.nhlbi.nih.gov/about/ncsdr

National Sleep Foundation
www.sleepfoundation.org

Restless Leg Syndrome (RLS)
www.rls.org

SleepNet.Com™
www.sleepnet.com

Smart Drivers Brake for Sleep
www.drowsydriving.cornell.edu

Publisher's note:
The websites listed on these pages were active at the time of publication. The publisher is not responsible for websites that have changed their addresses or discontinued operation since the date of publication. The publisher will review and update the websites upon each reprint.

Glossary

ASTHMA A condition often of allergic origin that is marked by continuous or paroxysmal (convulsive) labored breathing accompanied by wheezing, by a sense of constriction in the chest, and often by attacks of coughing or gasping.

BIOLOGICAL NEED Something necessary to sustain life and living processes.

CHRONICALLY Marked by being of long duration or frequent recurrence.

CHRONOBIOLOGY The study of biological rhythms (the rhythmical changes in biological functions of a plant or animal).

COMPROMISED Caused the impairment of.

CONSOLIDATING Joining together into one whole; uniting.

DEFICIT A lack or impairment in a functional capacity.

DEFECTIVE Imperfect in form or function; faulty.

EPIDEMIC An outbreak or product of sudden rapid spread, growth, or development.

EPILEPSY Any of various disorders marked by disturbed electrical rhythms of the central nervous system and typically manifested by convulsive attacks, usually with clouding of consciousness.

ERECTILE Relating to or capable of undergoing physiological erection.

INTRINSIC Belonging to the essential nature or constitution of a thing.

JUVENILE ARTHRITIS Youthful onset of inflammation of joints due to infectious, metabolic, or constitutional causes.

MUSCULAR DYSTROPHY Any of a group of hereditary diseases characterized by progressive wasting of muscles.

NEUROLOGIST A physician skilled in the diagnosis and treatment of disease of the nervous system.

PERCEIVE To attain awareness or understanding of.

PHILOSOPHERS People who seek wisdom or enlightenment; scholars, thinkers.

PRIORITY Something given or meriting attention before competing alternatives.

RECURRENT Running or turning back in a direction opposite to a former course.

REGULATION The state of bringing order, method, or uniformity to.

SABOTEURS Things that practice an act or process tending to hamper or hurt.

SEDATING Keeping a quiet steady attitude or pace; calming.

SEIZURE DISORDER Conditions such as epilepsy that are marked by sudden attacks (as of disease).

SPORADIC Occurring occasionally, singly, or in scattered instances.

STIMULATES Excites to activity or growth or to greater activity.

TRANSITIONAL Marked by passage from one state, stage, subject, or place to another; changing.

VALID Well-grounded or justifiable; being at once relevant and meaningful.

Index

Picture Credits

Artville pp. 10, 21, 22, 28, 34, 35, 46, 57, 66, 82, 104, 106, 117
Corel p. 53
Eti Swinford | Dreamstime.com: p 60
iDream Stock pp. 25, 40, 100
Image Source pp. 12, 15
Masterseries pp. 31, 50
Photodisc pp. 18, 36, 54, 65, 69, 70, 73, 74, 77, 78, 84 86, 89, 90, 112, 114,
Photos.com p. 93
Subbotina | Dreamstime.com: p. 118
Thinkstock p. 43

The individuals in these images are models, and the images are for illustrative purposes only.

To the best knowledge of the publisher, all other images are in the public domain. If any image has been inadvertantly uncredited or miscredited, please notify Vestal Creative Services, Vestal, New York 13850, so that rectification can be made for future printings.

Biographies

Joan Esherick is a full-time author, freelance writer, and professional speaker who lives outside of Philadelphia, Pennsylvania. Joan has contributed dozens of articles to national print periodicals, written spiritual and educational books, and speaks nationwide.

Carolyn Bridgemohan, MD, is a senior staff member of the Developmental Medicine Center, Children's Hospital, Boston, and instructor of pediatrics at Harvard Medical School, Boston. She specializes in assessment and treatment of autism and developmental disorders in young children. Her clinical practice includes children and youth with autism, hearing impairment, developmental language disorders, global delays, mental retardation, and attention and learning disorders. Dr. Bridgemohan is coeditor of "Bright Futures: Case Studies for Primary Care Clinicians: Child Development and Behavior," a curriculum used nationwide in pediatric residency training programs.

Dr. Sara Forman is a board certified physician in Adolescent Medicine. She has worked at Bentley Student Health Services since 1995 as a Senior Consulting Physician. Dr. Forman graduated from Barnard College and Harvard Medical School and completed her residency in Pediatrics at Children's Hospital of Philadelphia. After completing a fellowship in Adolescent Medicine at Children's Hospital Boston (CHB), she became an attending physician in that division. Dr. Forman's specialties include general adolescent health and eating disorders. She is the Director of the Outpatient Eating Disorders Program at Children's Hospital in Boston. In addition to seeing students at Bentley College, Dr. Forman sees primary care adolescent patients in the Adolescent Clinic at Children's and at The Germaine Lawrence School, a residential school for emotionally disturbed teenage girls.